BÔ YIN RÂ
(JOSEPH ANTON SCHNEIDERFRANKEN)

THE GATED GARDEN
VOLUME NINETEEN

LIFE'S
HIGHEST GOAL

For more information
about the books of Bô Yin Râ and
titles available in English translation,
visit The Kober Press web site at
http://www.kober.com/

BÔ YIN RÂ
(JOSEPH ANTON SCHNEIDERFRANKEN)

LIFE'S
HIGHEST GOAL

TRANSLATED FROM THE GERMAN BY
B.A. REICHENBACH

THE
KOBER
PRESS

BERKELEY, CALIFORNIA

For permission to quote or excerpt, write to:
The Kober Press
2534 Chilton Way
Berkeley, CA 94704

Email: koberpress@mindspring.com

This book is a translation from the German of
Das hohe Ziel, by Bô Yin Râ (J.A. Schneiderfranken),
published in 1925 by Verlag Magische Blätter, Leipzig.
The copyright to the German text is held by Kober Verlag,
AG, Bern, Switzerland.

Printed in the United States of America

International Standard Book Number: 978-0-915034-19-2

Typography and composition by Dickie Magidoff

Book cover after a design by Bô Yin Râ

The Kober Press
is highly grateful to
Alex Campbell
for donating his time, skills, and
imagination to design a web site that
clearly reflects the nature and
value of our publications.

CONTENTS

PREFACE

HIGHER THAN ALL GOALS IN LIFE ON earth remains the timeless goal this book's disclosures seek to show you.

In vain, however, will you seek to reach that goal if you assumed it to be somewhere far away.

The path that leads you to your highest goal is in yourself; and in yourself alone shall you one day attain your highest goal.

And likewise only in yourself will you receive all the support and help that you have need of on your path.

Only in yourself can you discern and grasp the helping hands that are prepared to guide you.

Do not mistake your merely having learned about the teaching that seeks to make you recognize the goal, and means to guide you to the path on which you can attain it, for having already entered the path in fact.

Not until you search within yourself according to the guidance of this teaching can it truly bring you blessings.

Within yourself you then shall also find the help you need.

If the words of this book are thus to guide you to your highest goal, you have to let their message echo in yourself.

You thus will in yourself discover that steep and narrow path; and if courageously you seek to scale it, then shall it one day let you reach your highest goal within yourself.

❧

CHAPTER ONE

THE CALL OF
THE SPIRIT

NOT WITHOUT GOOD REASON DID THE sages of the past repeatedly admonish that one should seek the Spirit in solitude and stillness, and to await the Spirit's call "behind closed doors."

What then can be discerned within is apprehended only by the soul, which purely through its feeling senses what words of human language are not able to express.

Blest are those who in this way can hear within, by virtue of their feeling.

NOT ALL will have the gift to hear the Spirit's call when first they try.

Often they will need to abide in "prayer" for some time before their inner sense shall open so that it will let them hear the Spirit's call within.

Even as the sound of strings played far in the distance allows only the trained and sharpened ear to recognize a melody, while others hear no more than disconnected notes, so also will the call of the Spirit be discerned by those alone who were able so to sharpen their inner hearing, and to attune the soul to the Spirit that it will know what it hears.

Deafened by the constant noises of the day, many stray without direction through the desert, patiently waiting for the call that might reach them, but unaware of their deafness.

In vain will the call of the Spirit endeavor to stir them.

Those by noise bewildered must first grow conscious of their deafness, so that in stillness they may regain their hearing.

If spiritual reality then reaches again their ears, they need to learn consistently to keep the turmoil of the outer world at bay, yet not to flee from its assaults.

Whatever might surround them in external life, within themselves they must at all times guard their stillness.

The tumult of the day must not disturb their inner life, even though without it rages with full fury.

Those who seek to hear the Spirit's call must listen for it only in themselves.

For only within themselves can they learn to comprehend what words have never expressed.

Having learned to listen within, no turmoil or noise will blunt their perception.

Amidst the outer world, whose pounding waves engulf them, they will be, for themselves, like islands of stillness.

The breakers' fury and the tempest's howling they will learn to disregard, and from the silence in themselves the Spirit's call will reach them.

ACTIVITY AND work will not disturb the stillness that is here required.

Not in the silence reigning in the realm of death can seekers ever hear the call within.

Only in the ebb and flow of life's domain will also inner stillness be imbued with life, from which the Spirit can beget what in the human being is of spiritual nature.

Solely what was thus begotten of the Spirit can hear the Spirit's call; for it alone may then reveal to human beings who they truly are.

Whoever seeks in other ways to hear his essence called "by name," is bound to wait in vain forever.

The call he longs to hear will not come from within until the innermost already has awakened, by virtue of the Spirit's power to beget, which manifests itself alone in stillness. Spiritual Reality is apprehended only through the innermost within.

THE TEACHING you are given from without is meant to serve as merely preparation.

It is to make your inner self aware of spiritual life, so that you one day will be able to recognize the call that from your innermost would reach you.

Such teaching will at all times tell you of the Spirit only what can be conveyed through words; the Spirit's ultimate Reality, however, reveals itself by virtue only of experience.

You cannot apprehend the Spirit's life except by your becoming one with it.

Turn, then, with all your energy toward that which is within you, and ask the Spirit in yourself to awaken your innermost from its sleep.

Abide in this "prayer" until your plea is heard.

Nurture stillness and confident serenity.

Not even your "prayer" must disrupt that stillness.

Even less must you impetuously demand what shall bestow itself on you without your asking, as soon as stillness has prepared your inner self.

Await your day in cheerful calm.

Be active in external life with all your strength and energies, but never let the worries of the outer world defile the tabernacle of your soul.

Within yourself you must at all times guard untroubled stillness, despite the storms that rage in outer life.

No strident sound of the external world must reach your inner self.

Thus, when your day has come, you shall discover your profoundest depth, and be uplifted to your loftiest height.

And so you will discern the Spirit's call within you, and recognize your own self in the Spirit.

Within the Spirit's life you then shall find your own life part of Life eternal.

ॐ

CHAPTER TWO

THE TWO PATHS

MORE THAN EVER BEFORE IS IT NECESSARY in this day to point out, again and again, that not everything "mysterious" in the world around us will lead to that most sacred, final mystery which alone can bring the soul fulfillment of eternal liberation.

Indeed, it may be necessary even to caution against taking this warning too lightly; for the confusion in some minds has reached such disturbing levels that, blinded in their exaltation, they no longer recognize the most explicit rejection of their folly, and blithely distort the word of warning into unreserved agreement.

For many years—indeed for decades, and long before the outbreak of the slaughter of nations, whose evil-laden atmosphere of bloodshed continues weighing like a cloud of guilt upon all life on earth—the Western world, proud of its knowledge and intellectual enlightenment, had fallen prey to an insidious pollution of its spiritual heritage, so that nowadays every hidden secret truth will find its satyr play and parody.

It truly is no wonder that seekers after knowledge follow paths that lead astray.

THE MESMERIZING glimmer enshrouding the mysterious border realms of human exploration has at all times cast its magic spell upon receptive minds, but seldom has the world seen such a lack of inner judgment as in our day.

As a moth is drawn to a flame, so is the inexperienced who remains without warning irresistibly attracted toward that fascinating phosphorescence from spheres of the unknown, but there he also faces the same danger and the same destruction.

Temptation flares from every kind of moldy crypt and storage bin of rubbish.

Deluded partial knowledge, half-educated folly, and calculated fraud are everywhere able to attract new groups of followers; and not a few have been beguiled whom one would surely not expect to find in such unwary company.

Yet at the root of all this lies a restless yearning, which all the knowledge of the age could never still; it only went so far astray because it was denied to find the right path on its own; for over-zealous pride of knowing has so completely blocked it that only darkest night still yawns where long ago one had been able to gain freedom.

Deeply anchored within human beings is the vague sensation of a higher world, in which they hope to find the answer that will solve the mystery of their existence.

This vague sensation is, however, nothing other than the distant, feeble recollection of their former spiritual state, before the "Fall" into the bondage here on earth.

They now seek to recover what they once had lost, yet in their search too easily fall prey to nether-worldly forces, which they do not see, although these long since have compelled them to obey their call; too late do seekers then discover that they had blindly mistaken the abysmal glow of destruction for the earthly likeness of the life-giving Light, which at first they had sought to discover.

All who feel the inner urge to find the answer that explains their lives' enduring mystery should therefore clearly bear in mind that there exist two paths, and that it will depend on solely their own prudence whether they will choose the proper one, which leads them to the goal they truly seek, or will in drunken rapture entrust themselves to the glistening path of delusion.

One of the two paths which they will see before them shall guide them to light and illumination, and finally into the radiance of the Spirit's realm, while the other, toward which they will be lured by tempting phantoms, which promise them both spiritual might and magic power, unfailingly will lead them to destruction—unless they get help through grace from above, and they recognize, before it is too late, that they had trusted an illusory light, which has nothing in common with the Godhead's radiance of purest gold and white, than the charm of being hidden to mortal human senses.

Not everything concealed, however, is worth to be explored.

Although the stars may be reflected even in a miry pond, one hardly would be digging through the mud in order to unlock their secrets.

In the same way, earnest seekers, moved by pure desire to find the Spirit's radiant substance in themselves, will surely not feel tempted to explore their future earthly fate; even if they can, and choose to, benefit from calculations, which, like other observations of this nature, indicate the tides affecting all they do, or leave undone, in physical existence, while they are alive and can be active here on earth, though in bondage to the energies that govern the material universe.

Here they would be wise to further what is useful, and to obstruct whatever might bring harm.

Yet they hardly will succumb to the delusion that a fate has been imposed on them which they cannot escape; instead, they will seek to unravel the rhythmic patterns of their lives only to employ this knowledge for the sake of avoiding what can be avoided, and to attract what will prove beneficial.

Already Paracelsus, fond of stating wisdom in his often ornamental style, spoke from knowledge when he expressed the insight, based on profound understanding,

"The stars wield no power whatever; they are free and on their own, even as we are free and on our own."

And likewise, "A child has no need of either star or planet; the mother is its star and its planet."

That is not to say, however, that the influence of cosmic energies in physical nature does not in fact exist. It merely was ascribed to the "stars" because their apparent motions allowed observers to determine the effects of that influence. It rather means that, notwithstanding its effects, the freedom purposefully to employ this influence remains entirely within ourselves, and in the discipline of our will; so that, equally, the calculation of latent possibilities will be beneficial only in the service of increasing self-control, and if it causes us to summon all our energies to liberate our lives from fear of the unsteady tides of currents that we cannot see. Currents that, although they constantly pervade all matter of the earth, are scattered at the adamantine dams, erected by the Spirit's might, protecting seekers having faith, who know to ask for such protection through their deeds.

Nor will such seekers bow to the oracular pronouncements that present the future's changeable potential as inexorable fate; indeed, they hardly will pay heed to such ideas.

Even less will they condone that, for the sake of probing the unknown, one turns human beings into tools of nether-worldly forces, and thus increasingly deprives them of the power to use their bodies' senses.

Nor shall they ever seek to make others relinquish control of their will in order to subject them to their own.

In everything they do and leave undone they serve exclusively the freedom which alone the Spirit's children truly know.

Every phenomenon of physical nature, every event of this life on earth can be turned toward either good or evil; and showing human beings how to use this ability at all times in the proper way is the aim of all the teachings of those who guide with authority.

"Not he that says to me, 'Lord, Lord' will enter the kingdom of heaven, but he that lets his own resolve be guided by the will of Him who, as my Father, brought me forth."

Words expressing this were spoken once by one who had authority to teach, since owing to his spiritual experience he knew of what he spoke. And of himself he thus could truly say,

"I do not teach from myself, but as the 'Father' commanded me, even so, so I teach you."

But the wisdom of this Luminary, the greatest transfigured by Love, had been reshaped in all too earthly ways before it reached the present age, which now can hardly recognize its pure original message.

What his teaching meant to show, however, was nothing other than the way how mortal human beings can learn to use their earthly lives to work toward their "salvation" by virtue of their deeds.

ALL MERE knowledge about the things of quite unequal value that lie beyond the reach of the body's physical senses produces nothing more than sterile pseudo-insights. It never leads to freedom from the yoke of earthly bondage.

Only the sober, action-inspiring resolve, which genuine insight awakens, can accomplish the wonder of liberation, if it is able to turn what is revealed to the soul into effective activity; and all one may teach in words will ever gain value only if such teachings shall lead to experience.

Blessed are who thus attain experience in themselves, and in their innermost then reach the goal to which alone the right path truly guides.

༚

CHAPTER THREE

ON SEEKING
AND FINDING

IT TRULY IS MUCH EASIER TO POSTURE as a seeker probing the external world, and to uncover even its most hidden crypts, assured of fame for new discoveries, than in oneself to find one's innermost; for this remains concealed to even those who think the energies that form the soul have long been analyzed so thoroughly that to their eyes the soul itself dissolved into a nebulous nonentity.

You therefore would do well to bid your pride be silent, despite your having gained astounding knowledge where even the wisest minds of the past faced only dark enigmas.

Besides, you likely may consider many an enigma "solved" only because you content yourselves with solutions that embody nothing of the depth from which the ancients heard enigmas whisper questions.

Also among the seekers of the past were those who knew how to find; and if like them you intend to succeed, you must prepare yourselves to seek where they had truly found.

I shall help you seek within yourself, for there alone can you expect to find what has been sought in every age; and in yourself it will become your own.

Neither by thinking, nor by logically impeccable deductions can you ever gain the knowledge that finally will solve the many questions seeking answers that continue to confront your soul; questions that keep rising from the dark of physically confined perception.

Forbid, therefore, all noisy thoughts in you to speak; so that within you there is nothing but the solemn silence that is not disturbed by any voices coming from without.

Then, however, learn the crucial art of waiting, in fullest confidence and trust.

To learn this art is anything but easy; yet all who later found what they had sought first needed to have mastered it. And no one can be spared this effort who hopes to find the knowledge that he seeks.

If you intend to find, resist the temptation to shorten the time of waiting!

If foolishly you should succumb to this temptation, your time of waiting would only be made that much longer.

INDEED, WHOEVER entered this path in order to seek, but did not find what he had hoped to discover, may be certain that his efforts failed only because he brazenly believed he had the power to shorten the time of silent waiting.

As long as seekers still are prone to this belief, they have not yet attained the solemn inner quiet, which is the fundamental precondition for finding anything within.

What right, then, have they to complain that all their efforts led to nothing?

Also those who in this outer world would find what is concealed will seek in vain unless they can preserve the kind of inner quiet, which even in this outer realm is needed, if they are to discover what they seek.

But all who ever sought the key to final things within their innermost, and there had found what they desired, first had practiced the art of waiting, and thereby fostered a culture of stillness within.

Only in silently knowing their innermost depth were they granted what thousands had sought in vain, given they lacked inner stillness.

"The kingdom of heaven tolerates force, and only the forceful make it their own."

This "force," however, is nothing other than the energy of self-control, which banishes all restlessness far from the soul.

Not until you have created such stillness in yourself that you would think it foolish even to wonder when you shall attain illumination are you truly close to fulfillment; and then you may be confident that you indeed will find what was concealed to you when, still in bondage to impatience, all your labors were in vain.

You must regard it as entirely irrelevant when here on earth you shall attain the highest light of knowledge. You ought to seek like someone whose search is not confined by any limits of time.

You have to seek like someone who is sure of finding, because he knows that what he looks for does exist, and cannot hide from him as soon as he is worthy to attain it.

The more your inner certainty increases, together with the confidence in your own self, the closer also will you be to helpers from above.

Nurture faith and confidence within yourself, and banish the corrosive thoughts that time and again would subject you to fear, as if you were not destined to find what you seek.

Learn to comprehend that yielding to such fear is blasphemy!

Within yourself you carry the key to freedom from all doubt, and only in yourself can final certainty become your own.

Rid yourself of everything that would subvert such faith in your own self, even if until this day you had accepted it as "sacred truth."

Within the innermost, where you are to be granted final insight, all mental intellection must fall silent, even if it had been venerated for thousands of years.

You there shall be alone with your own self; nor is there any might on earth that either could obstruct you, or help you to succeed.

Nowhere save within your innermost can you expect to find what you are seeking; and weighed against what here is to become your own, all the wonders of the starry universe will then appear to you as merely dust and nothing,

Within your innermost shall you discover your own self; and only then will you at last see clearly that the aim of all your restless searching was in truth—yourself.

෴

CHAPTER FOUR

THE RADIANCE OF ETERNAL LIGHT

DARKNESS FELL UPON HUMBLE DWELLINGS, and palaces lie under gloomy clouds of dismay.

One searches for oil lamps to fend off the darkness and candles are lit on the candelabra, but the darkness will not give way.

IN TRUTH, there is need of a different light if joy is again to enter your lives.

But, my friends, if only you show trust in its power, that different light will certainly conquer the darkness around you.

You are not aware that your own will holds you in bondage to the darkness.

Be not afraid of the darkness that everywhere covers all paths around you.

You have turned yourselves toward darkness, so that night must now surround you, until its time has passed, and you resolve to turn yourselves again toward light.

Yet even the dark is a herald that promises light.

It awakens energies that make you long for light, and thus your will is stirred to turn around.

Practice patience, and firmly abide in confident trust!

Before long, the light of the sun will surely again shine on your path.

Even in the depth of darkness is timeless light no farther from you than in brightest radiance, if only you are willing to turn yourselves toward its brightness.

Turn to face the light, and all the darkness shall be left behind you.

That is how the sages of old entered the light, joyful in strength, and left what belonged to the darkness behind them.

Their heirs, however, felt more and more attracted by the allure of darkness.

What lay behind them they thought more important than the path ahead they were meant to pursue.

And so they learned to keep their eyes trained on the past, and directed their steps toward what lay behind them.

In the dark they hoped to find what reveals itself only in light.

But you, the late descendants of these heirs, should thus not be surprised that darkness now surrounds you; for, following the misdirected steps of those in earlier days, you still are tempted to stay turned toward darkness.

You will have to turn around if, like the ancients sages, also you would find yourselves encompassed by the light of the sun.

This reversal calls for courage and for firm resolve of will.

Your eyes have long been unaccustomed to the light that can alone return you one day to enduring joy.

At first you now will find the sunlight painful, until your eyes grow strong enough to bear it, and then will learn to love its rays.

YET MANY today are close to turning around, and not a few have truly done so already.

None will here be left without guidance, if only he dares to turn back on his own.

You that now still seek by moving backwards, abandon the paths of error, which only lead you deeper into darkness.

And you that long since have grown tired of all seeking, do not content yourselves with merely lighting wretched tapers in your palaces and huts!

Have the courage to turn around to face eternal light, and leave the darkness behind you!

Bear this in mind: Light and Darkness forever remain at the place which is theirs.

You alone decide whether you choose to bear the bondage of unending darkness, or will confidently turn your eyes toward light.

Be assured: Eternal Light will shine upon you one and all.

❧

CHAPTER FIVE

THE COLORS OF ETERNAL LIGHT

THE LIGHT OF THE ETERNAL SUN comprises countless colors, and only few in any age have come to know the fullness of its radiance.

To nearly all others, excepting those few, it reveals only one of its numberless aspects.

Mere willfulness can here not change what cosmic law imposes.

Your eye alone determines the color in which you are to see the light.

You may stand in the midst of light, and yet be unable to see it, as long as you would force your eye to show you the light in a color that is not uniquely your own.

You thus can persuade yourself to believe in any illusion, while moving ever farther away from light, and yet assume you are approaching it.

Recognize that I guide you well; for it is the fulfillment of my temporal life to offer good guidance to all who will hear me.

To you, then, my counsel is this: Do not falsify your own color, nor desire to see things of a coloring different from that which one day is to become your own.

You cannot attain any real knowledge of truth except in your own individual color.

Only when you observe yourself very carefully will you also be able to recognize your own individual color.

But it truly is not necessary that you discern it beforehand, as long as you shall willingly entrust yourself to your guidance, and not attempt to determine the color yourself in which the light of eternity is to approach you.

It is established within yourself, from all eternity, in which color the light is able to bring you its blessings.

It is established within yourself what your eyes shall one day behold.

You are to have trust in yourself, and must learn to show faith in your innermost.

Be mindful, to be sure, of what others were granted to behold, and thus discern in everything they may disclose to you the infinite bounty of light, but clearly remain at all times aware that you—whoever you may be—are destined to witness different aspects, even though all colors always display but the selfsame light.

To you it will be able to reveal itself only according to your given nature; and everyone's nature is different.

As long as you still seek to discover the light within you as it appears through another's potential, you merely prevent it from reaching you in your own given color; but then you should not be surprised if you find that others are conscious of light, while you continue to grope in the dark.

CERTAIN TEACHINGS you were given told you that the selfsame light shall one day shine on all who strive on earth for timeless light; and such teachings indeed are rooted in the fruitful soil of truth.

It is prudent to trust such teachings; one also needs to know, however, that the selfsame light pours forth its colors in infinite rays, so that it may reach thousands upon thousands, and still shall bestow itself on each in a color that differs from all others.

The self-revelation of light is unique in time and essence in each of us; and everyone receives illumination in solely his own way.

Still, those who in themselves received the light know clearly that its radiance is the very same whose rays became effective also in their fellow seekers, who had like them been granted light.

None had received a different kind of inner light, but each beholds the selfsame light in a different color.

Infinite riches thus lie enshrined in light everlasting.

IF ONLY I could convey a reflection of the infinite riches of light to all of you striving to reach it—as do plants given shelter in cellar rooms during the winter!

If only I could, in words of human language, disclose to you the inexhaustible wealth of your spiritual heritage!

Yet too well I know that temporal words are doomed to remain a hapless stammer if they attempt to express eternal reality.

I here can do no more than try—like someone who had witnessed wondrous things on a long journey into distant lands—to call forth images of that which you have never seen; but if you would within yourself behold what I convey, you must be willing to pursue the path whose goal shall let your own eyes clearly see, within your inmost self, and fully conscious of the splendor that I here can promise you.

Whether in this world you are revered as someone possessing wisdom, or judged to have but little worldly knowledge, recognize that you are certain to attain eternal light if only you resolve to seek it in yourself.

Fend off beguiling voices tempting you to seek eternal light as beheld through the eyes of others!

Seek it instead in yourself, and according to your nature, bearing in mind that only in your individual color you one day shall behold it; be it that you can accomplish this already in your life on earth, or only after you at last had to surrender this mortal body to its fate of decay.

Confidently enter and pursue your path according to your nature; and whatever in your own way you may hope to encounter shall be far surpassed by what is one day to become your own.

CHAPTER SIX

ON THE NATURE OF
THE HIGHEST GOAL

IN TRUTH, THE PATH THAT LEADS YOU to your highest goal is long, and steep, and rugged; but once you recognize what lies in store for you at the end of that path, no goal that any other path this life on earth might have to offer will seem to you of even vaguely comparable worth.

A treasure is waiting for you at the end of your path, which no one but you can ever possess.

Even though countless seekers will here be granted the same immortal prize, for each who has attained that highest goal there is a treasure waiting that only he can raise.

No one else can here possess what you alone are able to attain.

You need to come yourself if you would raise that treasure.

Failure to do so amounts to abandonment; for in all eternity none but yourself can become that treasure's owner.

Comprehend what that implies!

Become aware and clearly discern the worth embodied within you.

You that seek life's highest goal, recognize that you are able to know spiritual reality only after you have gained objective certainty that both the path, and the goal of that path, are found within yourself alone.

Solely in your inmost self can you attain the lofty goal of which these words would make you conscious and aware.

Within your innermost you bear a hidden treasure that no one else can ever take from you.

Only your own folly can here deprive you of what is most exclusively your own.

At this I see you tremble and succumb to fear; yet you truly would misread my words if you should feel afraid the obstacles that rise between you and your goal are certain to defeat you.

Yet only fearless courage will let you achieve your goal; the very goal that keeps itself concealed within you.

Bear in mind, my friends, that the attainment of even the loftiest goals in outer life on earth is child's play, while heroic is the labor that achieves the timeless goal one bears within.

In outer life, others may prevent you from reaching a goal that you want to attain; here, by contrast, you only face obstacles of your own making within you.

You can clear your way of any obstacle, if this is your earnest will; and help from above shall then lend strength to your resolve.

But however ardently you might be seeking spiritual help, you shall remain beyond its reach until your will is active in the same direction in which such inner help is to advance your quest.

You need to, as it were, become a *magnet* for such help, if you are to attract it on your path.

The powers that offer such help do not willfully act by choice; for all their ability to grant support is limited by organically functioning laws.

Much as waves of electrical energy deliver messages of many different kinds through physical space, but are not able to reach you, until they encounter an instrument that is able to detect them, even so is spiritual help at all times at your side, without your being conscious of its presence; unless, that is, you will transform yourself into a spiritually sensitive "receiver" that can detect the wave length of such spiritual help.

Once organically connected to that timeless help, you have no further need to worry or to fear, but shall with certainty attain your highest goal; be it already in this present physical life, or only after you were granted to give this mortal body back again to the earth.

Your highest goal is reaching the perfection of your timeless self, such as its form is born within the Spirit.

In all eternity no other can attain the spiritual perfection in the form that is uniquely yours.

Although within the lower realms of physically experienced nature you frequently find members of a species being so remarkably similar that there appears to be no difference between them; yet also here, examination of the higher forms will soon reveal that each succeeding rank displays increasing multiplicity of individuations, which even inexperienced eyes can hardly overlook.

Similarly, there is differentiation of kinds within the Spirit's realm.

There are, as it were, "lower" kinds, which, glanced at in passing, appear to be alike in individuation; and there are likewise higher, and the highest kinds, whose individuations become increasingly dissimilar.

But no matter to which kind you may yourself belong, bear in mind that in yourself you are from all eternity immutably defined, and individually differentiated from all others forming part of the same kind.

Although, in general terms, the lofty goal you are to reach remains the same that shines on all who in the wellspring of eternity are born out of the Spirit, even so the form in which you shall be able to attain that goal is different from that in which all others shall attain it.

From all eternity you bear within yourself the form, born only once within the Spirit, which now is solely yours, and which no other can attain in all eternity, even though it may not come to be your own for aeons.

PERHAPS YOU have already for some time been on the path to reach your highest goal, but to this day have still not found it because you sought to make another's highest goal your own?

You failed to have sufficient trust in your own self and thought that you could only find through others what might be worth the effort of your quest.

You did not recognize that thus you would yourself become your enemy.

You did not know that you had sinned against yourself by your attempt to make another's highest goal your own.

Make atonement to yourself for your sins, today, as you are reading these words, and henceforth only seek within yourself the highest goal that none but you is able to attain.

Even if your highest goal may still conceal itself in distances beyond your reach, and though today you scarcely may be able to envision it, as heavy clouds of haze still hide it from your view, you nonetheless have gained incomparably more than if all others' highest goals were readily within your grasp.

Only having reached the highest goal that is uniquely yours will you achieve perfection.

Only being able to find the goal that is your very own have you in truth attained life's highest goal.

In this quest you are yourself at once the bow, the arrow, and the highest goal.

You are to reach the highest spiritual perfection of your being.

No God can liberate you from your chains as long as you, within yourself, still do not clearly see your highest goal before your eyes, which is in truth:

> your TIMELESS SELF
> in union with your God.

❧

CHAPTER SEVEN

ON THE PATHS OF
THE ANCIENTS

O N YOUR QUEST TO SEEK THE PATH to Light, which is the path that leads you to yourself, it would be foolish to assume that path could only be pursued according to the ancients' practice.

But it likewise would be foolish and presumptuous if in your own day you were to look upon the distant ancients' paths with condescension.

Truly, those who lived and toiled on earth before you were also able to seek and to find, and many a treasure they found which those who came after them lost again.

You can only benefit if you learn to reflect on the paths of the ancients with an open mind and free of common prejudice.

They had discerned profoundly hidden secrets, whose knowledge later generations sought to recover in vain; knowledge also your contemporaries judge to be forever enigmatic.

Learn to regard the ancients with reverence if in your own days on earth you seek to attain lasting knowledge.

No one has ever been born on this earth who achieved inner knowledge, but did not stand on the strong shoulders of others who had gone before him.

Fools in every age have always craved sensational "novelties," yet in the end, the law of procreation was at all times subject to the same conditions.

Also you shall never gain objective knowledge of your timeless spiritual being except in ways that are essentially similar to those of the ancients, even though the form this quest will take is bound to vary in the course of time.

Every age has its distinctive form of seeking and of finding, but if you search for the enduring essence in all forms you easily will recognize that it remains the same in all its variations.

Also you should therefore seek in only the form that accords with your time, and not be tempted to search in the guise of old and borrowed costumes of the past.

You would no more than play the hero in a masquerade, convinced you are performing mighty deeds while strutting on the stage, if thus you sought to make the ancients' form you own, and in their ways to prove your worth.

You cannot find unless you seek in your uniquely given form, which always will accord with your own time.

Whoever counsels you differently will lead you into error, even if he does not know that his advice obstructs your path.

THE SAGES of each epoch sought in their own way, and in the form of seeking that accorded with their time.

Thus they found what they had sought.

But they also knew to honor the ways of seeking and finding of those who preceded them; and far from their mind was the error of thinking the earlier seekers were foolish.

Much in ancient accounts may strike you as inscrutable only because you no longer can fathom their language.

Other parts may be confusing because they speak of things in words you know, but which today one would no doubt express in different terms.

Still other things had been intentionally entrusted to hermetic diction, so that the real meaning of the words can barely be detected, in that their sense was to reveal itself to only those who clearly knew the key to understand that way of speaking.

Thus the actual paths of the ancients are buried to you in manifold ways, and only intuitively can you sense that these paths had truly led to the goal; to the very goal that also you are seeking to reach.

A PERILOUS undertaking is the attempt to recover these thoroughly buried paths and to make them again passable in this day.

Very few are able to remove the covering debris completely, but even if this should succeed, all traces of the path then suddenly appear so blurred that any effort to go further relies on random speculation.

If you truly would become a pupil of the ancient sages, you always must, as they had done, pursue no other path than that which your own day has opened for your quest.

The ancient sages, too, were children of their time, and even though they honored the paths their fathers had pursued, they understood full well that, like the fathers, they could only reach the goal by following the path that was their own.

Also you should honor the paths of the ancients, but do not labor to uncover them under all the debris; for whatever you might unearth would always be merely traces of paths that others had gone. And thus you shall truly never discover the path that is yours.

ॐ

CHAPTER EIGHT

ON THE BLESSINGS
OF WORK

THERE ARE COUNTLESS INDIVIDUALS IN OUR days who strive for the unfolding of their spiritual nature; and even though many devour any disclosure of timeless spiritual insights only to give desired satisfaction to their insatiable curiosity, far more of them must be regarded as earnest seekers after truth.

As pilgrims they set out to visit every sacred spring; and any site where wondrous events are said to have occurred they look upon as holy.

From the written heritage accumulated through the ages, dusty tomes are brought to light in which one hopes to find precise instruction on how the realm of miracles can be connected to the everyday; for it has long been known that lofty energies are to become attainable to those who apprehend the Spirit's timeless laws.

One may surely smile at the folly of those who would learn to become sorcerers' apprentices; yet many who fervently strive toward the Spirit are not by any means immune to foolishness; and not a few believe that they can only apprehend the Spirit if they submit to an external schooling, requiring peculiar exercises, the stranger the better.

And so they randomly accept first this, then that instruction, found in old or modern books, in which an enterprising mystagogue, with gestures indicating secret insights, publishes his muddled wisdom, taking pride in dark pronouncements.

Whenever one crosses their path, they invariably have just discovered the definitive recipe to distil the philosophers' stone in their private alembic.

The only thing for which one must admire them is being able to pass from one disappointment to another, without ever losing the peculiar courage to let themselves be hoodwinked by the next deception.

It often may take long before they recognize that in this way the goal they seek to reach remains forever unattainable.

With difficulty only do they learn to understand that it in fact betrays appallingly defective judgment to hold the highest and most sacred wisdom in such low regard as to believe that one could reach by means of breathing exercises, in all but dislocated postures, and other, still worse practices, confusingly directed by befuddled minds, what the wisest of all ages had venerated as the holiest of gifts.

Yet mortal man is all too readily inclined to bow before the wondrous strange.

Much rather would he follow confusing, maze-like alleys his eyes cannot survey, and, deluded by his folly, let himself be lured into the dark, instead of entering the straight and solid path toward light, in order to pursue it in wide awake sobriety and steadiness; even as a wanderer who carefully observes the path's direction, in order that he one day shall indeed achieve his goal.

ONE DOUBTLESS must be strong to walk the journey toward a distant goal, and those who would not falter from exhaustion before they have arrived, will also make provisions for nourishment along the path itself.

Likewise, the path to the Spirit requires strength, and renewal of energy, from all who intend to pursue it.

But here they have no need to venture far afield, nor to look for questionable alley ways to find the required refection.

The life of the everyday will offer it abundantly if one knows how it ought to be lived.

But here again there are not many who realize how highly must be valued the energy that is engendered and renewed through work that is in all respects well done.

One rather would indulge in lofty dreams, and therefore looks on work as a disrupting hindrance on one's path; as a distraction of one's progress, and best to be avoided.

But those who assume the highest goal may be attained this way will surely not attain it; even if the wisdom of all the sages of the world were known to them from books, and they at any time immersed themselves in feelings of sublime elation.

It is much easier to denigrate the duties of one's everyday than truly to fulfill them.

It is much easier in fancied consecration to feel that one is "close to," or even "unified with," the Spirit of God, than to perform one's work in such a way that it becomes a source of strength for one's own spirit, which thus grows able to be consecrated in reality.

The values that lie here concealed are truly worth attaining.

You surely have seen acrobats performing at a circus and were amazed and full of admiration to see how people like yourself had here so perfectly developed, and made subject to their will, the powers of their bodies that they were able to accomplish things which would to you be utterly impossible.

From their example you can learn a lesson.

Even as they had developed their bodies' potential only by virtue of endless practice, so can you today draw unimagined spiritual energies from work of any kind which you are able to perform so well that no one could do better.

Even as those acrobats performing in the circus must concentrate with full attention on every movement of their hands, on every motion of their bodies, if their act is to succeed and not expose their lives to gravest risk, so, of course, must also you perform your work, in all things it demands, if you expect it to bear spiritual fruit; that is to say, with such attention as if your life depended on every movement of your hands.

Whether your mind or your hands are primarily engaged in your work, there will always be any number of such actions, routinely performed, almost unconsciously from habit, "purely mechanically," the value of which you thus diminish yourself.

As a result, you naturally will find them boring and monotonous.

But in the same way as those daring acrobats, whose work appears to you more like a cheerful game, are forced to, again and again—every evening which calls them to perform the selfsame work before an eagerly watching public—to focus on the slightest movement of their muscles, because the same display of their skills might fail in tonight's performance, although it had succeeded yesterday, so you as well must recognize that even the same routinely performed motion always becomes something new, no matter how often you may have performed it.

HOWEVER "MONOTONOUS" and spiritually "benumbing" your work might appear to you, consider it from that perspective and do not lower it still more in your esteem. You then will either discover how its monotony may be relieved, or you will perform the same activity your work demands of you each day, with ever new awareness, so that your spirit will detect a thousand new and different aspects in the same "routine."

Accustom yourself to performing your work with joy, even though it seems by no means apt to make you joyful.

Overcome your aversion, and you will prove superior to even the most tedious work; it will bring you joy by virtue of the way you master it.

If the order of performing chores is something you decide, begin with what you dislike most, and force yourself to love it.

Having overcome your foremost aversion, and shown yourself the stronger, will of itself become a source of satisfaction, and also make the rest of your labors more joyful.

You must never regard your work as purely a means that needs to be used to acquire your life's daily necessities.

Here is where most people's thinking is in error.

To be sure, every work is worthy of its wages, and you burden yourself with guilt by serving another who unjustly seeks to withhold what he owes you, being indebted to you for the worth of your labor.

However, that which is yours as the fruit of your work is strictly determined by spiritual law.

You burden yourself no less with guilt if you accept more for the worth of your labor than it increases the wealth of the one who employs you; and here you must never forget to what extent the other in turn is directly involved in the work you perform.

Yet all the external compensation for your work remains a pittance when compared to what your work may let you gain in spiritual values if you will treasure it as work performed for its own sake.

Well done work contains its highest value in itself; and this enduring worth cannot be taken or withheld from you by anyone.

Even in the humblest kind of work one may endeavor to attain perfection; and if it is attained, by means of total dedication to one's labor, the natural consequence will always be an unimagined increase in one's spiritual energy.

The worker standing day after day at a machine, where his only task consists in turning out screws, may thus bring forth within him spiritual energies of priceless worth, while someone else who, in his view, lives only on exalted spiritual planes, but pays far more attention to the raptures of his inner life than to the quality of the work he is expected to perform, in one way or another, remains completely empty-handed, and unknowingly deceives himself if he believes his spiritual strength is growing.

In order to obtain the spiritual energies that can be gained through work that strives for highest excellence in performance, it is not necessary that the work as such should be devoted to some spiritual end.

Yet while the enduring fruit of labor will thus consist in a continued growth of spiritual energy, it would nonetheless be folly to disregard the other benefits, which disciplined work of this kind will also contribute to everyday life.

Most people still do not recognize the effect of such work for daily life, even though countless examples might teach them.

Solely work performed for its own sake—work that strives for the highest perfection is able to create the widely desired state of general wealth, which can never be achieved so long as work is merely endured as a distracting necessity.

Those do not know of the blessings of work who still have not learned that work can be loved.

Those will never enjoy the blessings of work who dream of a happiness wherein work plays no part.

⚭

CHAPTER NINE

THE MIGHT OF LOVE

THE MIGHT OF HUMAN BEINGS TRULY knows no limits when their lives embody love.

Love truly is the human being's highest power here on earth.

Lofty powers have been celebrated as the human mortal's highest merit, and his greatest glory was envisioned high on soaring peaks; far higher renown, however, than mortals themselves could imagine has been prepared for their glory; and farther than their thoughts' most daring flight could ascend have they been granted power.

The heavens cannot encompass what fiery might of love, awakened in hearts of mortals on earth, is able to accomplish; nor can it ever be uncovered, in all the depths of Being, where the consecration anchors which causes animal-like creatures to be divinely transformed into human beings born in the Spirit.

Suns disintegrate in cosmic tides throughout the aeons, tearing worlds with them into the void of fathomless extinction; the might, however, that is granted human beings remains their own for all eternity, even though the ground on which in earthly time they built their dwellings may shake and burst apart beneath their feet.

They, who once had fallen from the realm of timeless light, even now retain the might within to raise themselves beyond the highest stars.

You ask what source bestows such might on them, even though they once had fallen?

You ask what raises them above the hosts of unseen princes ruling in the hidden world of physical creation?

Recognize that final clarity can here not be conveyed by words of human language; for only feeling intuition can discern what may be felt, but never apprehended by the mind.

How, then, could any human tongue reveal what must remain beyond all mortal intellection?

Even to those lofty potentates that rule the astral spheres, who are by nature purest intellect—although immeasurably superior to any physical capacity of forming thoughts—to those invisible "gods" of visible reality, remains eternally concealed what only human souls are able to behold and to experience within their inmost selves.

Far above these astral gods' all-powerful control of life unfolding in the cosmos will human might ascend when it is rooted in the ground of love.

It has been said, "God is love, and he that dwells in love, dwells in God, and God in him."

But what you mean by "love" became too closely linked with physical desire, a pleasant sense of passion-driven feelings; and rather than dwelling in "God," you yourself erected the idol you serve on your knees, but which has no power to help you. Prudent minds, aware of this delusion, thus turned their back on it; and now you claim they are "denying God," because they dare to question and reject your idol's "godhead."

But I can tell you that more than one who thus has turned away from idols and from gods may be far closer to the godhead than those who revile him.

I can tell you that many of those you regard as "deniers" of God truly found refuge in God's protection and, dwelling in love, experience God; even though their way of speaking may differ from yours, and they themselves may not be aware of dwelling in God, and that God is manifest in them.

For: "God is Spirit, and those who worship Him must worship the Truth in Spirit."

Those who fail to seek the Spirit within them will not find God in all eternity.

To be sure, the Spirit that is God, and Love, must not be equated with the "spirit" which minds of mortals, born of dust, are able to fashion by thought.

We here are speaking of a different kind of Spirit; and those who do not feel its grace through love, will needs remain godless, no matter how much they are able to say about God.

Solely in the Spirit's form of Love can mortal human beings ascend to God, and thus into the Spirit, from which they had descended, issued by the Word of Life, which speaks itself in God throughout the aeons without end.

Before that goal is reached, all the human mortal's rhapsodizing on "God" and things divine is simply idle chatter, and all his praying, unless it be rooted in love, is for nothing.

He that once had taught you to pray as one ought to pray, not merely to prattle, like those who are far from God's realm, he wanted to see you awake in that love.

Indeed, his very life was a lesson revealing that love.

How can you expect to understand him while you still hesitate to lose yourselves within the same eternal fire, and in it to surrender all your being, in order to regain yourselves anew within that love?

THE LOVE to which I here refer can never be entirely attained so long as you still need an object for your love that you must seek outside yourself.

You must yourself become the object of that love, until at last you also lose yourself within it, and thus behold yourself transformed to love that has no need of any object, as everything that ever was, or is to be, remains enclosed within it.

If, wisely counseled, you are taught to renounce your very soul, you need to understand this simply to mean that not even your soul should become the object of your love, if truly you desire to know the love that will reveal God's light within you.

If you would make your own, through "love," things other than what in your inmost being strives to apprehend its timeless *self*, your "love" is still confined by narrow earthly bonds, far from the living essence which manifests a spiritual aspect of the Godhead.

You, however, are to find the love within you that is God; and you are to be in this love, that God may be in you, and you in God.

You still have no true "being"; for what you speak of as your "self" is not a "being" that is conscious of its own enduring "self."

What you consider as your "being" is "being" only by analogy; much as that which you regard as "love" is "love" in merely that related sense.

What you refer to as your "being" is subject to a thousand influences, much as love dependent on its object always is conditioned by something that remains outside, however highly you may elevate it in your thought.

Above, beyond, and higher than all such reflections must I raise you, if I truly am to lead you to the Love wherein your God is born in you, and you in Him.

Only those ascend to realms above who "rise up" in themselves, and consciously resist all lower drives that seek to hold them fettered to the ground.

Indeed, it is already a "rebellion" against all lower instincts when you seek an object for your love, because you here intuitively sense that you must firmly stand against all lower influences if you are to master them.

As long as you still seek the object of your love outside yourself, however, you cannot find your timeless inner ground; and thus you should at first *yourself* become the object of your love.

Having thus grown conscious of your inner ground, it will be easier for you to surrender even that last support, in order to "rise up" against yourself, until you reach the sphere where neither height nor depth exist, since all comparisons to space are without meaning; for mysteries beyond all likeness here form themselves into events.

COMPREHEND: the heavens are unable to contain the wealth that lies in store for human beings who do not fail to claim what is their own.

It is true that, after aeons, all shall finally attain a state of "bliss"; the "bliss" which all shall one day get to know cannot, however, be compared in any form to that most lofty goal you can achieve if you resolve, already in your mortal time of life, courageously to raise yourself to inner heights, and find the strength to free yourself from bondage to the unseen rulers of the cosmos; bondage that may hold you captive for millennia, and aeons.

Concerning that, however, it was said that "No one shall gain freedom until the uttermost farthing has been paid."

Today, however, it is still within your power to wrest yourself from that bondage.

Today you are still able to become the master of your fate; and those among your Brothers here on earth, who long since have become such Masters, know of no greater joy than being permitted to offer you their help.

ช

CHAPTER TEN

THE MASTER
OF NAZARETH

"AND THOUGH I SPOKE WITH THE TONGUES of men and of angels, but had not love, I would simply be like a sounding brass and a tinkling cymbal."

Those are the words of one who knew of love and its power.

Yet before him there had been another; one who revealed that love in his life's eternally radiant teachings.

While he — in our midst we call him *the greatest of all transfigured by love* — had been anticipated by many of his spiritual Brothers, none before him had attained the fire of love he embodied.

And many had lived after him, and many are still to appear, whom one may truly call transfigured by love; and yet, for all the power of their love, there never has been one, nor could any still be born, who might become his equal. And here I speak of those who are his Brothers, with whom he is One in the Spirit.

What had revealed itself before him, through each of his spiritual Brothers, was the same at all times; but in him its revelation reached fullest abundance.

And all that in the course of time is still to be revealed will likewise be ever the same; merely the form it will be given shall be different and new.

Only thoroughly benighted minds are able to assume that the figure of the carpenter from Nazareth is simply the invention of a pious myth. However, the historical personality whom later ages have come to know only in an image that, centuries after his life on earth, sought to portray his temporal appearance, was truly anything but the fakir-like worker of miracles into which he was turned at a time when superstitious faith of Eastern and Western thinkers had long been struggling to give shape to his portrait and nature.

Those who in this construct truly would detect the trace of fact must learn to purge the image that, from childhood on, they had revered as sacred, of all the foreign matter inserted by miracle-craving generations, their minds in bondage to the earth.

Then only will the Master's radiant eye behold them, and they shall see the countenance of one who—unified with God in the profoundest sense—had also, as a human being, brought "glad tidings" to his fellow beings, telling them about a realm of Spirit, of immortal living substance, of which he spoke as the "kingdom of heaven."

If I here speak of "others," including myself, as being his spiritual Brothers, all would quite mistake my words who were to think we others meant to resemble the earth-withdrawn magician's image, to which later ages attached the name of the carpenter from Nazareth, seeking to make him the equal of the "Logos."

Such foolishness is far from us.

Those who, through their questionable skills, endeavored to enthrone him firmly in the highest place of heaven, instead have merely estranged him from all mortal human nature, thus raising him beyond the reach of those he sought to guide to the Spirit's highest realm.

No wonder that to them he would at last become a myth.

Believe me, friends, I know full well what I am saying when here I refer to the greatest of all transfigured by love as the exalted Brother.

None of us, no matter to what heights the Spirit may have exalted him, would ever indulge the insanity that he—the speaker—were the primordial Word *itself* that is speaking through him. We therefore deem it a blasphemous defamation to believe that he, the greatest of all transfigured by love, had taken pride in such blatant insanity.

We want to show him to you as he truly was, when he, like us, still bore the burdens of this life; such as he even now—united in the Spirit as the Brother of his Brothers—is manifest to us, each single day, one with us and visibly apparent in his timeless spiritual form.

When we, who hold him in profoundest veneration, call ourselves his Brothers, this simply means that, as a human being on this earth, he had been one of us; and also that he, in his spiritual identity, continues to be one of us; notwithstanding that the Son of Man, who had experienced all things human when he lived on earth, would later, in a now quite distant, miracle worshipping age, become transformed into the "God," who needed to descend from his divine eternal glory because a small, old nation's vengeful idol allegedly could not contain his wrath, but for the sacrifice of his own "son."

WE DO NOT speak of someone whom we know from merely dark, uncertain legends.

We are united with the one of whom we testify in ways no earthly form of union is able to connect one human being with another.

We know, even if we did not otherwise, through him to whom this chapter is devoted, that in his day, when as a human being living on this earth, he was in all respects like one of us, a human being. By virtue solely of his radiant might of love did he so utterly surpass us all that he was able to perform the miracle transcending every earthly measure, through which he so transformed the spiritual aura of this planet that henceforth every mortal guided by "good will" can find the path back to the Spirit, which is Love; for now that path is cleared and marked, so that none can go astray; even as a wanderer walking through heavy snow cannot miss the road that was "plowed" by one who knew the way.

The guidance that here reaches you through our words is thus in truth what he himself had taught.

If you observe that we are marked by human traits, even though we must declare ourselves to be his spiritual Brothers, bear in mind that also he, like us, had been a human being, and that no human feeling was beyond his own experience.

Nothing in human life did he hold in such low regard that he failed to share it himself.

He never would have been the one he was, had not the wealth of all things human found room to manifest itself in him.

Nor, for that matter, was it in his power to dis-entangle himself from this encumbrance with human nature, had he wanted to escape it.

Solely that he rose triumphant in the end ac-counts for his surpassing greatness; even as all those who seek to follow him can prove themselves as "chosen" only if they are able to look upon the follies of this earth, which they can never wholly escape during mortal life, as ultimately being *nothing*; and if they learn to rid themselves of all imaginary "guilt of sin," so that in Light of Liberation they may rise, their innermost consumed in the radiant fire of the love that in the Master, with whom they can become united only through love, had brought about the timeless wonder of his life.

ALL THEY that hope to find, within their being's innermost, the greatest of those trans-figured by love—for he truly is so close to all who live on earth that finding him is easy— above all else must learn to set aside the deluded belief that was able to turn the purest human being ever to have lived on this earth into the "God," who sacrificed himself to satisfy the irate thirst for vengeance of his

"Father-God," whom all too human zealotry invented.

Only then shall they within themselves discern the presence of the radiant Master: the carpenter sage from Nazareth.

✧

REMINDER

"Yet here I must point out again that if one would derive the fullest benefit from studying the books I wrote to show the way into the Spirit, one has to read them in the original; even if this should require learning German.

"Translations can at best provide assistance in helping readers gradually perceive, even through the spirit of a different language, what I convey with the resources of my mother tongue."

From "Answers to Everyone" (1933), *Gleanings*. Bern: Kobersche Verlags-buchhandlung, 1990

Other Works by Bô Yin Râ published in English translation:

Bô Yin Râ:
An Introduction to His Works

Contents: Preface. About My Books. Concerning My Name. In My Own Behalf. Essential Distinction. Résumé. Comments on the Cycle <Hortus Conclusus> and the Related Works. Brief Biography of Bô Yin Râ. The Works of Bô Yin Râ.

The Kober Press, 2004, 117 pages, paperback. ISBN 0-915034-10-7

This book presents a summary of the essential features that set the author's works on final things apart from the innumerable publications, old and new, that seek to answer questions which thinking minds have asked in every generation. Traditionally, such answers draw upon beliefs, accepted faith, and speculative thought, culminating in systems of religion and philosophy. Rarely have solutions rested on objective insights into the dynamic structure of reality, embracing both its physical and spiritual dimensions. But in addition to providing such direct descriptions of these aspects of reality, the author's books are helpful guides that let the readers gradually develop their inherent faculties so that they may experience this reality themselves. For readers having sensed the nature of this ultimate experience the concepts "spirit," "soul," "eternal life," and "God" are then no longer merely abstract notions based on hope and faith, but have become realities that form the human being's timeless essence, even as they underlie all aspects of creation.

In the first chapter of this *Introduction* the author discusses the origin and purpose of his books; how they should be used; for whom they are intended, and what their application may accomplish. Here he also stresses that his writings neither are opposed to, nor written to support, any particular religious creed, even though the followers of all persuasions may benefit from what they have to offer to all who seek to know.

The following chapter sheds light on the author's name and explains why his books are published under this spiritual proper name, which is not an arbitrary pseudonym, invented for the purpose of effective self-illumination, but expresses, in phonetic equivalents, the essence of his nature.

In the final chapter he corrects a number of misunderstandings of his books and person, typically prompted by hasty judgments, hearsay, or prejudice. Here he also touches on the common source of all authentic spiritual disclosures and stresses that objective insights into that dimension ought to be distinguished from the subjective mystical visions found in the different forms of religion.

The Book on the Royal Art

The Kober Press, 2006. 198 pages, paperback. ISBN 0-915034-13-1

This work is the first volume of *The Gated Garden*, a cycle of thirty-two books in which the author shows the way that lets his readers find objective spiritual truth within the light that darkness cannot conquer. In this opening volume the author discloses his own spiritual origin and sources and explains the reason leading to the publication of these books in our time. As the Western mediator of the oldest roots of ancient Eastern wisdom he also gives his readers the criteria to distinguish spurious echoes of that wisdom.

Of particular significance for Western readers is the chapter "The Night of Easter," which recalls the actual events preceding what would later be accepted as the Resurrection. In this context the book also touches on the Eastern wellspring in the teachings of the historical Master of Nazareth.

The concept "Royal Art" in the book's title refers to the Indian Raja Yoga, but here the term is used to denote a spiritual craft that far transcends the practices that are today suggested by that name.

As the portal to *The Gated Garden* this book is of particular importance in that is sets the tone and outlines the perspective from which all other volumes in the cycle should be viewed and understood.

The Book on the Living God

Contents: Word of Guidance. "The Tabernacle of God is with Men." The "Mahatmas" of Theosophy. Meta-Physical Experiences. The Inner Journey. The En-Sof. On Seeking God. On Leading an Active Life. On "Holy Men" and "Sinners." The Hidden Side of Nature. The Secret Temple. Karma. War and Peace. The Unity among Religions. The Will to Find Eternal Light. Mankind's Higher Faculties of Knowing. On Death. On the Spirit's Radiant Substance. The Path toward Perfection. On Everlasting Life. The Spirit's Light Dwells in the East. Faith, Talismans, and Images of God. The Inner Force in Words. A Call from Himavat. Giving Thanks. Epilogue.

The Kober Press, 1991. 333 pages, paperback. ISBN 0-915034-03-4

This work is the central volume of the author's *The Gated Garden*, a cycle of thirty-two books that let the reader gain a clear conception of the structure, laws, and nature of eternal life, and its reflections here on earth. The present work sheds light on the profound distinction between the various ideas and images of "God" that human faith has molded through the ages —as objects for external worship—and the eternal *spiritual reality*, which human souls are able to experience, even in this present life. How readers may attain this highest of all earthly goals; what they must do, and what avoid; and how their mortal life can be transformed into an integrated part of their eternal being, are topics fully treated in these pages.

What sets this author's works on spiritual life apart from other writings on the subject is their objective clarity, which rests upon direct perception of eternal life and its effects on human life on earth. Such perception is only possible, as he points out, if the observer's *spiritual* senses are as thoroughly developed to perceive realities of timeless life, as earthly senses need to be in order to experience *physical* existence. Given that authentic insights gathered in this way have always been extremely rare, they rank among the most important writings of their time, conveying knowledge of enduring worth that otherwise would not become accessible

The Book on Life Beyond

Contents: Introduction. The Art of Dying. The Temple of Eternity and the World of Spirit. The Only Absolute Reality. What Should One Do?

The Kober Press, 2002. 161 pages, paperback. ISBN 0-915034-11-5.

This book explains why life "beyond" is not so much a different and wholly other life, but rather the continuation of the self-same life we live on earth. The difference between the two dimensions lies chiefly in the organs of perception through which the same reality of life is individually experienced. On earth we know that life through our mortal senses, in life beyond it is perceived through spiritual faculties, which typically awaken after death. At that transition, the human consciousness, which usually is unprepared for the event, is at a loss and finds itself confused by the beliefs and concepts of its former mortal life. As a result, the new arrival faces certain dangers; for, owing to these mental prejudices, the person is unable to distinguish between perceptions of objective truth and the alluring phantom "heavens" generated by misguided faith on earth.

To help perceptive readers form correct and realistic expectations, that they may one day reach the other shore with confidence and without fear, this book provides trustworthy guidance into spiritual life, its all-pervading structure, laws, and inner nature. Given the unbreakable connection between our actions here on earth and their effects on life beyond, the book advises how this present life may best prepare the reader for the life that is to come.

The Book on Human Nature

Contents: Introduction. The Mystery Enshrouding Male and Female. The Path of the Female. The Path of the Male. Marriage. Children. The Human Being of the Age to Come. Epilogue. A Final Word.

The Kober Press, 2000, 168 pages, paperback, ISBN 0-915034-07-7

Together with *The Book on the Living God* and *The Book on Life Beyond*, *The Book on Human Nature* forms a trilogy containing guidelines toward a new and more objective understanding of both physical and spiritual realities, and of the human being's origin and place within these two dimensions of creation.

The Book on Human Nature at the outset shows the need to draw a clear distinction between the timeless spiritual component present in each mortal human, and the material creature body in which the spiritual essence is embodied during mortal life. The former, indestructible and timeless, owing to its being born of spiritual substance, represents the truly human element in what is known as mortal man. The latter, physical, contingent, and subject to decay and death, is no more than the temporary instrument the spiritual being uses to express itself in physical existence. Given that the spiritual and animal components within human nature manifest inherently discordant aspects of reality, they typically contend for domination of the total individual. Experience shows that in this conflict the animal component with its ruthless drives and instincts clearly proves the stronger.

To help the reader gain a realistic understanding of the human being's spiritual and physical beginnings, by way of concepts more in keeping with humanity's advances in every discipline of natural science, the book explains, to the extent that metaphysical events can be conveyed through language, the timeless origin and source of every human's spiritual descent. It likewise shows that the material organism, now considered mankind's primal ancestor, existed long before it was to serve the spiritual individuation as its earthly tool. In this context the author points out that the traditional creation story, such as it has survived, is not simply an archaic myth, invented at a time that lacked the benefits of modern knowledge, but instead preserves, in lucid images and symbols, a truthful view of actual events. Events, however, that did not happen merely once, at the beginning of creation, but are a process that continues even now, and will recur until this planet can no longer nurture human life.

Even so, the principal intention of the present work, as well as of the author's other expositions of reality, is not so much to offer readers a new, reliable cosmology, but rather to encourage them to rediscover and awaken the spiritual nature in themselves, and thus to live their present and their future life as fully conscious, truly human beings.

The Book on Happiness

Contents: Prelude. Creating Happiness as Moral Duty. "I" and "You". Love. Wealth and Poverty. Money. Optimism. Conclusion.

The Kober Press, 1994. 127 pages, paperback. ISBN 0-915034-04-2.

Sages and philosophers in every age and culture have speculated on the nature, roots, and attributes of happiness, and many theories have sought to analyze this enigmatic subject. In modern times, psychology has joined the search for concrete answers with its own investigations, which frequently arrive at findings that support established views. Still, the real essence of true happiness remains an unsolved riddle.

In contrast to traditional approaches, associating happiness with physical events, the present book points to the spiritual source from which all human happiness derives, both in life on earth and in the life to come. Without awareness of this nonmaterial fundament, one's understanding of true happiness is bound to be deficient.

The author shows that real happiness is neither owing to blind chance, nor a capricious gift of luck, but rather the creation of determined human will. It is an inner state that must be fostered day by day; for real happiness, as it is here defined, is "the contentment that creative human will enjoys in its creation." How that state may be created and sustained, in every aspect of this life, the reader can discover in this book.

The Path to God

Contents: Fantasy and Faith. Knowing Certainty. Dreaming Souls. Truth and Reality. Yes and No. The Decisive Battle. Individual Perfection.

The Kober Press, 2008. 129 pages, paperback. ISBN 978-0-915034-15-8

While the author's *Book on the Living God* provides a comprehensive overview and introduction to spiritual realities affecting human life on earth and, in the chapter "The Inner Journey," describes the path that leads the human soul to the experience of life's final mystery, the present work outlines a number of essential aspects that readers need to bear in mind as they pursue that path.

As it is of critical importance that the reader's mental concepts correspond, as far as human language permits, with facts of spiritual reality, the book draws clear distinctions between the powers of authentic faith in something that in fact exists, and the innumerable phantoms human minds invented and imposed as objects of belief.

Likewise, in the spiritual domain the concept "knowledge" does not signify the mere accumulation of countless random facts, but rather the ability to comprehend the object to be known by virtue of becoming one with its reality.

The chapter "The Decisive Battle" sheds light on the mysterious entity whom Jesus defined as the "prince of this world," and refers to the destructive influence of that purely temporal being and its place in the physical cosmos.

The path to God illuminated in the book is not the search for an object of emotional worship, but instead, as summed up in the book's concluding sentence, the journey to each seeker's individual perfection in the Ground of Being.

The Book on Love

Contents: Introduction. The Greatest of Compassion's Mediators. On Love's Primordial Fire. Light of Liberation. On Love's Creative Power.

The Kober Press,. 2005. 148 pages, paperback. ISBN 978-0-915034-12-3

Love, properly understood, is not merely, as the author explains, a human sentiment of varying degrees of intensity, inspired by particular objects and, like all feelings, subject to continuous change. Love is, instead, the highest of creation's elemental powers, giving life to and sustaining all dimensions of reality. The human sentiment called "love" is but a faint reflection of that cosmic force and ought to be distinguished clearly from its distant source.

Earthly love in all its forms is typically aroused by the desire of possession for an object. Celestial love, by contrast, is a spiritual energy that manifests itself beyond and free of all desire, independent of external objects. Human beings can partake of the celestial form of love, which then transforms their temporal existence by virtue of their timeless life, and thus will make them more than simply "sounding brass and tinkling cymbals."

In its initial chapter the book sheds light on the historical facts surrounding the life and teachings of the unprecedented figure of Jesus of Nazareth, who, more perfectly than anyone before or since, embodied love's celestial force in word and deed. Empowered by that highest form of love he found the strength to change this planet's spiritual aura in his final hour and freed all human beings of good will from ancient bondage.

The Book on Solace

Contents: On Grief and Finding Solace. Lessons One Can Learn from Grief. On Follies to Avoid. On the Comforting Virtue of Work. On Solace in Bereavement.

The Kober Press, 1996. 126 pages, paperback. ISBN 0-915034-05-0.

In this book the author shows how sorrow, pain, and grief, although inevitable burdens of this present life, can and ought to be confronted and confined within the narrow borders of necessity. Considered from the spiritual perspective, all suffering experienced on this earth is the inexorable consequence of mankind's having willfully abandoned its given state of harmony within the Spirit, a deed that also ruined the perfection of material nature. Although the sum of grief thus brought upon this planet is immense, human beings needlessly expand and heighten its ferocity by foolishly regarding grief as something noble and refined, if not, indeed, a token of God's "grace."

Understanding pain objectively, as a defect confined to physical existence, which, even in exceptional cases, is but an interlude in every mortal's timeless life, allows the reader to perceive its burdens in a clearer light, and thus more patiently to bear it with resolve.

While suffering, through human fault, remains the tragic fate of physical creation, the highest source of solace, which helps the human soul endure its pain and sorrow, continually sends its comfort from the Spirit's world to all who seek it in themselves. How readers may discover and draw solace from that inner source the present book will show them.

The Book of Dialogues

Contents: Testimony. Knowledge and Reality in Action. Light and Darkness. The Spirit's Might. The Jewel of the Heart. Transformation. The Dialogue on the Innermost East. The Dialogue on the Passing of a Master. The Flower Garden. The Deviant Pupils. Night of Trial. Individuality and Person. The Realm of the Soul. On Finding Oneself. On the Elder Brothers of Mankind. Mystery of Magic.

The Kober Press, 2007. 175 pages, paperback. ISBN 978-0-915034-14-X

This book contains a series of conversations between the author as a pupil and his spiritual mentors, before he was himself accepted as a Master in their circle. It touches on a number of essential topics that help the reader recognize authentic knowledge of objective spiritual truth and the nature of those who, since the dawn of time, have conveyed that truth to humankind as spiritually sanctioned Mediators.

The book is of especial interest for its biographical disclosures, as these not merely shed unprecedented light on the development and schooling of authentic spiritual Mediators, but also on the singular position assigned to the author of the present and the other volumes of The Gated Garden.

As the Western representative and voice of the perennial Eastern source from which all timeless insights into spiritual light and knowledge flow, the author shows the way to those who have been guiding human spirits to eternal light since ages immemorial, long before the rise of temporal religious creeds.

While insights from that highest source have reached humanity in ancient days, time and misinterpretations have shrouded their authentic form, nor have they ever been presented to the public at large as an integrated whole in such detail before.

The Wisdom of St. John

Contents: Introduction. The Master's Image. The Luminary's Mortal Life. The Aftermath. The Missive. The Authentic Doctrine. The Paraclete. Conclusion.

The Kober Press, 1975. 92 pages, clothbound. ISBN 0-915034-01-8.

This exposition of the Fourth Gospel is not a scholarly analysis discussing the perplexing riddles of this ancient text. It is, instead, a nondogmatic reconstruction of the actual events recorded in that work, whose author wanted to present the truth about the Master's life and teachings; for the image propagated by the missionaries of the new religion often was in conflict with the facts. The present book restores the context of essential portions of the unknown author's secret missive, which the first redactors had corrupted, so that its contents would support the other gospels.

Written by a follower of John, the "beloved disciple," its purpose was to disavow the "miracles" the other records had ascribed to the admired teacher. His record also is unique in that it has preserved the substance of some letters by the Master's hand, addressed to that favorite pupil. Those writings are reflected in the great discourses which set this gospel text apart and lend it its distinctive tone.

Given the historic impact of the man presented in this work, an accurate conception of his life and message will not only benefit believers of the faith established in his name, but also may explain to others what his death in fact accomplished for mankind.

The Mystery of Golgotha

Contents: Introduction, The Mystery of Golgotha. The Most Pernicious of Our Foes. Love and Hatred. The Soul and Its Growth. Spiritual Guidance. Occultists' Exercises. Mediumism and Artistic Creation. At the Wellspring of Life. Membership in "The White Lodge." Follies of Imagination.

The Kober Press, 2011. 228 pages, paperback. ISBN 0-915034-18-5.

In the present book, as in *The Book on Love* and in *The Wisdom of St John*, the author states that the spiritual work accomplished at Golgotha was a cosmic event that profoundly changed the spiritual aura of the planet. Ever since that day all human beings of "good will," in search of timeless light and liberation, no matter what their faith might be, including also "non-believers," are offered the gift of being able to attain the highest spiritual goal that human beings can pursue in life on earth. Symbolically, the conquest of Golgotha has been has been described as the defeat of the "prince of this world."

The author also explains that Jesus of Nazareth, while born in Galilee, was neither a teacher of the Jewish Law, which he merely cited on occasion, nor the founder of a faith that used his name and sayings to create a new religion that worshiped his as "God," but that his wisdom and authority derived from a higher source, of whose existence only myths and rumors have reflected knowledge until now.

The book also offers criteria to distinguish genuine and spurious teaching on spiritual reality, and emphasizes that intellectual proficiency should not be mistaken for conscious spiritual life.

The Meaning of this Life

Contents: A Call to the Lost. The Iniquity of the Fathers. The Highest Goal. The "Evil" Individual. Summons from the World of Light. The Benefits of Silence. Truth and Verities. Conclusion.

The Kober Press, 1998, 126 pages, paperback. ISBN 0-915034-06-9.

This book addresses the most common questions people tend to ask at times when circumstances in their daily lives awaken their awareness of the many unsolved riddles that surround the human being here on earth. To be sure, philosophy and teachings of religion have offered answers to such questions through the ages, but as these often draw on speculation, or require blind belief, they can no longer truly satisfy the searching mind of our time.

It is against this background that the present book will guide its readers to a firmer ground of understanding, resting on objective insights and experience. From this solid vantage, readers may survey their own existence and its purpose with assurance.

As this book explains, the key to comprehending the meaning of this present life is, first, the insight that this life is but the consequence of causes in the Spirit's world and, thus, has of itself no meaning other than that fact. And, secondly, the recognition that material life is ultimately meaningless if human beings fail to give it meaning: by virtue of pursuing goals whose blessings shall endure. The nature of the highest goal that mortals can pursue provides the substance also of the present book.

Resurrection

Contents: Preface. Resurrection. The Wisdom of Sages. Effects of Law and Chance. Wasted Labors. Mardi Gras of the Occult. Inner Voices. The Magic Effect of Fear. The Limits of Omnipotence. The New Life. Festive Joy. The Virtue of Laughter. Self-Conquest. Conclusion.

The Kober Press, 2009. 179 pages, paperback. ISBN 978-0-915034-16-1.

The sacred concept "Resurrection," historically associated with the Master of Nazareth, who had affirmed "I am the resurrection and the life," has through the centuries been faithfully misunderstood as the resuscitation of his dead and buried mortal body. The present book explains that the event of which he spoke was not a physical but spiritual transformation, which can, and ought to, be attained by human beings even in this present life. This *spiritual* reawakening is independent of religious creeds, but solely the result of conscious actions, thoughts, and words

What the "resurrection" of the spiritual consciousness within the human being's animal nature presupposes is the foremost subject of all the writings of this author. Here he discusses in particular some common misconceptions that prevent or hinder the attainment of this goal. At the same time he provides the reader with instructive guidelines that are helpful on this inner quest.

Worlds of Spirit
A Sequence of Cosmic Perspectives

Contents: Preface. The Ascent. The Return. Reviews of Creation. Epilogue.

Illustrations: *Emanation. In Principio erat Verbum. Lux in Tenebris. Te Deum Laudamus. Space and Time. Primal Generation. Seeds of Future Worlds. Emerging Worlds. Birth of the External Cosmos. Labyrinth. Desire for External Form. Astral Luminescence. Sodom. Inferno. De Profundis. Revelation. Illumination. Fulfillment. Victory. Himavat.*

The Kober Press, 2002. 96 pages, 20 full-color illustrations, hardcover. ISBN 0-915034-09-3.

If all the books of Bô Yin Râ, objectively considered, are unparalleled in the extensive literature on subjects touching final things—in that their author did not publish speculations based on faith or thought, but gave the reader fact-based insights into spiritual reality—the volume *Worlds of Spirit* occupies a special place even among these thirty-two unprecedented works; for in this book he integrated twenty reproductions of his paintings, representing *spiritual perspectives*, to illustrate selected aspects of his text.

While the works of the *Hortus Conclusus* cycle constitute the first authentic, comprehensive exposition of metaphysical realities, the paintings in this volume represent, in turn, the first objective visual renditions of spiritual dimensions in their dynamic figurations, colors, and inherent structure. Together with the written word—the book describes events experienced and perceived by an awakened human spirit—the images are meant to offer readers lucid concepts of nonphysical existence, and thereby to assist them in developing their own perceptive faculties.

On Prayer

Contents; The Mystery of Praying. "Seek, and You Shall Find." "Ask, and You Shall be Given." "Knock, and It Shall Be Opened Unto You." Spiritual Renewal. Let This Be Your Prayer: Twenty-Two Prayers.

The Kober Press, 2010. 138 pages, paperback. ISBN 978-0-915034-17-8.

In this book the author clarifies the fundamental difference between appeals addressed to an imagined God, who lives by only his believers' faith, and thus cannot fulfill their many wishes—and real prayer, which unifies the human spirit's will with the objectively existing wellspring of all Being, whose Mediators offer help and guidance to all who learned the sacred art of praying.

As the book explains, praying is an art one can and needs to learn, so that what is requested may be heard and answered. This learning brings about a transformation of a person's inner life, and leads to heightened spiritual self-awareness.

While there are limits to what prayer can effect in mortal life, it remains an indispensable source of strength and renewal in physical existence. Its highest gift, however, is the help it offers human beings on their way to conscious spiritual life.

Spirit and Form

Contents: The Question. Outer World and Inner Life. At Home and at Work. Forming One's Joy. Forming One's Grief. The Art of Living Mortal Life.

The Kober Press, 2000. 108 pages, paperback. ISBN 0-915034-07-7

The underlying lesson of this book is that all life in the domain of spiritual reality, from the highest to the lowest spheres, reveals itself as lucid order, form, and structure. Spirit, the all-sustaining radiant *substance* of creation, is in itself the final source and pattern of all perfect form throughout its infinite dimensions. Nothing, therefore, can exist within, or find admittance to, the Spirit's inner worlds that is devoid of the perfection, harmony, and structure necessarily prevailing in these spheres.

Given that this present life is meant to serve the human being as an effective preparation for regaining the experience of spiritual reality, this life must needs be lived in ways that are consistent with the principles that govern spiritual reality; in other words, ought to be lived according to the structure, laws, and inner forms of that reality. To show the reader how this present life receives enduring form, which then is able to survive this mortal state, the book sheds light on crucial aspects of this physical existence and advises how these may be formed to serve one's spiritual pursuits.

THE
KOBER
PRESS